W9-BWT-945

# FESTIVE FOODS

# GERMANY

Sylvia Goulding

CHELSEA CLUBHOUSE

An Imprint of Chelsea House Publishers

**Chelsea Clubhouse**
An imprint of Chelsea House Publishers
132 West 31st Street
New York, NY 10001

**Library of Congress Cataloging-in-Publication Data**

Goulding, Sylvia.
  Festive foods / Sylvia Goulding. – 1st ed.
    v. cm.
  Includes bibliographical references and index.
  Contents: [1] China – [2] France – [3] Germany – [4] India – [5] Italy – [6] Japan – [7] Mexico – [8] United States.
  ISBN 978-0-7910-9751-9 (v. 1) – ISBN 978-0-7910-9752-6 (v. 2) – ISBN 978-0-7910-9756-4 (v. 3) – ISBN 978-0-7910-9757-1 (v. 4) – ISBN 978-0-7910-9753-3 (v. 5) – ISBN 978-0-7910-9754-0 (v. 6) – ISBN 978-0-7910-9755-7 (v. 7) – ISBN 978-0-7910-9758-8 (v. 8)
  1. Cookery, International. 2. Gardening. 3. Manners and customs. I. Title.
  TX725.A1G56 2008
  641.59–dc22

                              2007042722

**For The Brown Reference Group plc:**
**Project Editor:** Sylvia Goulding
**Cooking Editor:** Angelika Ilies
**Contributors:** Jacqueline Fortey, Sylvia Goulding
**Photographers:** Klaus Arras, Angelika Ilies,
  Emanuelle Morgan, Dirk Scholz
**Cartographer:** Darren Awuah
**Art Editor:** Paula Keogh
**Illustrator:** Jo Gracie
**Picture Researcher:** Mike Goulding
**Managing Editor:** Bridget Giles
**Production Director:** Alastair Gourlay
**Editorial Director:** Lindsey Lowe
**Children's Publisher:** Anne O'Daly

**Photographic Credits:**
**Front and Back Cover:** Klaus Arras
**Fotolia:** 6; **Ewald Gerlach:** 8, 13; **Michael Gerlach:** 7; **Thomas Gerlach:** 22, 23, 39; **Mike Goulding:** 31; **Peter Hillebrand:** 20/21; **iStock:** title page, 34; **Shutterstock:** 3, 5, 6, 9, 10, 12, 13, 26, 28, 29, 30, 37, 38, 40, 41, 42

**With thanks to models:**
Anouk, Caspar, Gero, Jamila, Simon

**Cooking Editor**
*Angelika Ilies* has always been interested in cookery and other countries. She studied nutritional sciences in college. She has lived in the United States, England, and Germany. She has also traveled extensively and collected international recipes on her journeys. Angelika has written more than 70 cookbooks and cooking card series. She currently lives in Frankfurt, Germany, with her two children and has spent much time researching children's nutrition. Both children regularly cook with their mother.

# Contents

# let's START COOKING

Cooking is fun—you learn about different ingredients and cooking methods, you find out how things taste, and you can serve to your family and friends a meal that you have cooked yourself! Some of the recipes in this book have steps that need adult help—ask a parent or other adult if they will be your kitchen assistant while you cook a meal.

This line tells you how many people the meal will feed.

In this box, you find out which ingredients you need for your meal.

## WHAT YOU NEED:

### SERVES 4 PEOPLE:

2¼ cups white rice
4 eggs, beaten
light soy sauce
4 tablespoons
  groundnut or
  soy oil
2 green onions
⅓ cup peeled shrimps
⅓ cup ham
⅓ cup green peas

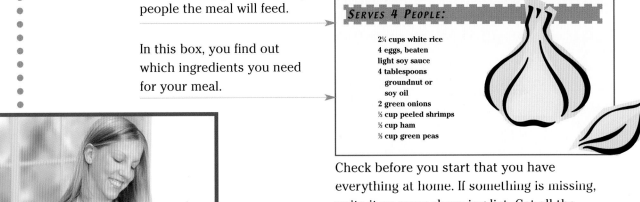

Check before you start that you have everything at home. If something is missing, write it on your shopping list. Get all the ingredients ready before you start cooking.

◁ I enjoy preparing all the fresh vegetables. I wash, trim, peel, and deseed them, if necessary. Then I slice and chop them all to the same size.

## ! WHEN TO GET help

Most cooking involves cutting ingredients and heating them in some way, whether frying, boiling, or cooking in the oven. Each time you see this exclamation mark, be extra careful as you cook and make sure your adult kitchen assistant is around to help.

For many meals you need to chop an onion. First cut off a thin slice at both ends. Pull off the peel. Cut the onion in half from end to end. Put one half with the cut side down on the chopping board. Hold it with one hand and cut end-to-end slices with the other hand. Hold the slices together and cut across the slices to make small cubes. Make sure you do not cut yourself!

For other recipes in this book you need to make a dough. Put the ingredients into a bowl and knead them with very clean hands or with the kneading hooks of a handheld whisk. In many cases, the recipe then tells you to cover the bowl with a clean cloth and to leave it in a warm place. During this time, the dough rises, that is, it gets bigger. After rising, knead the dough again until smooth.

A **barbecue** is not essential, but in summer German people enjoy cooking their meals outdoors.

**Oven gloves or mitts** are essential in any kitchen. Wear them each time you touch a dish on the stove or in the oven.

**Pepper mills** are a useful tool to have in any kitchen, because pepper tastes much better when it is freshly grated.

A **rolling pin** is a useful kitchen tool for rolling out the dough when you are making cakes, breads, or cookies.

# A trip around
# GERMANY

After World War II (1939–45), Germany was divided into two countries. In 1990, West Germany and East Germany reunited to become one state again.

**G**ermany is in the heart of Europe. It is a little smaller than the U.S. state of Montana and is divided into sixteen federal lands. Germany borders the North Sea and the Baltic Sea in the north. Its northern border with Denmark crosses a spit of land called Jutland. Germany's western neighbors are the Netherlands, Belgium, Luxembourg, and France.

▽ **About 82 million people** live in Germany. About ten percent of these are immigrants. They came from Turkey, Greece, Italy, Poland, Russia, Serbia, Croatia, and Spain.

Switzerland and Austria are to the south, and the Czech Republic and Poland in the east.

Northern Germany forms part of the North European Plain. In the center of the country, the land becomes hillier. In the south, it rises higher still in the Bavarian Alps. The Rhine is Europe's longest river and busiest waterway. It flows through the west of the country, from the Swiss Alps to the North Sea. In the east, the Elbe River crosses Germany to the Baltic. Many industries are located in a heavily built-up region around coalfields in the east.

NORTH
AMERICA

ASIA

EUROPE — GERMANY

AFRICA

◁ *Germany* is a large country in west-central Europe. Its population is the largest in the European Union. It shares borders with nine other countries.

**1**

△ *Sandy beaches* line the Baltic and North Sea coasts. The beaches in the east are quiet. Straw baskets protect people from the sea breeze.

DENMARK

BALTIC SEA

NORTH SEA

**1**

Hamburg

Elbe

LÜNEBURG HEATH

POLAND

**GREAT BRITAIN**

NETHERLANDS

Hannover ●

**GERMANY**

**3**

BERLIN ●
*SAXONY*

Dresden ●

**4**

**2**

BELGIUM

Cologne ●
Bonn ●

Rhine

**2**

Leipzig ●

**4**

CZECH REPUBLIC

△ *Cochem Castle* is a fairytale castle on the Moselle River. It is 1,000 years old.

● Frankfurt

*BAVARIA*

Stuttgart ●

Danube

Munich ●

△ *Dresden* is the capital of Saxony. It was once the residence of the kings of Saxony. The Zwinger *(above)* is a complex of pavilions and galleries built in 1711–22.

**FRANCE**

SWITZERLAND ⟶ LIECHTENSTEIN

AUSTRIA

SLOVAKIA

HUNGARY

SLOVENIA

CROATIA

◁ *Berlin* is the capital of Germany. It is located in the east of the country, about 100 miles from the Polish border. The Brandenburg Gate is one of its best-known landmarks. It once stood on the border between east and west.

**3**

BOSNIA-HERZEGOVINA

ITALY

*MEDITERRANEAN SEA*

## Northern Germany

Germany has many beautiful sandy beaches. On the North Sea coast, large mudflats appear when the tide goes out. A string of small islands, the East and North Frisian Islands, are just off the coast. Germany's largest island is Rügen on the Baltic coast.

The rolling northern plain contains marshes and moors, dotted with lakes and ponds. There is fertile soil for farming toward the uplands farther south. The large port of Hamburg stands on the banks of the Elbe River.

## Central Germany

The central uplands form a band across the middle of the country. The Harz mountain range is the most northerly mountain chain. Its higher slopes are covered with pine trees. The Main River winds its way across Germany until it joins the Rhine farther west. A cruise along the Rhine passes through spectacular

△ *A tall sailing ship* called a *windjammer* in the port of Hamburg during the Port Festival. Hamburg Harbor is the largest seaport in Germany and the second largest in Europe. Hamburg is located 69 miles inland from the mouth of the Elbe River.

scenery. In the Middle Ages (about 500 to 1500 CE), people built castles and fortresses here to guard and control this waterway.

On the terraced slopes of the Rhine, Main, and Moselle excellent vines are grown. Old volcanic craters in the Eifel Mountains are filled with bright blue water. Other mountain ranges include the Taunus near Frankfurt and the Erzgebirge on the Czech border.

## Southern Germany

The Black Forest takes its name from the dense, dark woods of pine and fir that cover its hills. It is a picturesque region in the southwest state of Baden-Württemberg. Tourists come here to enjoy the scenery and walking the tracks. The Danube River rises in the Black Forest and flows eastward across Bavaria.

The Bavarian capital, Munich, is famous for culture, food, brewing, and beer festivals. Lake Constance is a large lake on the Rhine, formed by a glacier many years ago. The Bavarian Alps are spectacular. The highest alpine peaks are in France, but Germany's highest mountain, the Zugspitze, reaches 9,718 feet.

▽ *Neuschwanstein Castle* near Füssen in Bavaria was built in the 19th century for King Ludwig II. It is Germany's most popular tourist site and became the model for Disneyland castles.

## LAPTOPS & LEDERHOSEN

*Bavaria is famous for its folk costumes. Men wear leather shorts or three-quarter length pants called lederhosen, women wear dirndls—dresses with white blouses and aprons. But there is much more to Bavaria than tradition. Big companies are based here, such as the automakers BMW and Audi, the engineering company Siemens, Airbus Industries, and many other high-tech companies.*

# The food we grow in
# GERMANY

Germany has short coastlines, but fruit and vegetables grow well, and rich meadows provide food for livestock.

**G**ermany is renowned as a country of meat eaters. But fruit and vegetables also grow well here, and people love locally grown and seasonal fresh foods.

## Northern plains

South of the North Sea and Baltic coasts, Germany has vast moorland areas. Here, sheep, honey bees, and berry bushes flourish. The Lüneburg Heath in Lower Saxony is especially famous for its heather honey. Lower Saxony's Altes Land is an important center for growing fruit. Sugarbeet, potatoes, and corn grown as cattle fodder are also important northern crops.

The city of Hamburg has market gardens nearby to supply it with fruit and vegetables, such as cabbages and carrots. In the southern part of the northern plains, the soil is more fertile. Wheat, barley, corn, and sugarbeet grow well here. There are also many dairy and poultry farms across northern Germany. The black-and-white Friesian cows are particularly famous. The farms often produce their own cheeses, sausages, and other products.

Germans are very fond of pickled vegetables—vegetables steeped in a mild vinegar with herbs and spices. The most famous pickle is sauerkraut (pickled white cabbage). Other favorites are gherkins (cucumbers of various sizes) and mixed pickles (carrots, peppers, and cauliflower).

## Central uplands

Highland soils are not as fertile as those found in river valleys, but farmers grow some cereal crops in upland areas. This region of the country is also good for growing potatoes and vegetables. Potatoes are very popular in Germany. They are boiled or used to make pancakes, salads, or fried potato dishes.

People keep pigs for pork products, such as ham and sausages. Dairy cows graze on hillside pastures, and beef cattle are reared for their meat. There are also small poultry farms that keep chickens, geese, and ducks.

Farming is intensive along the large and densely populated river valleys of the Rhine and Main. The land has to produce a large amount of food and so farmers often use fertilizers. But today people demand more and more organic food. Market gardens grow fruit and vegetables for people living in nearby cities, such as Cologne and Bonn.

◁ **Vast fields** of wheat, rye, and barley stretch across the plains in northern and eastern Germany. These cereals are ground and then used by bakers to make about 300 different types of bread.

Vines are grown in terraces along the steep, warm, protected hillsides of the Rhine, Moselle, Nahe, and Ahr rivers. They produce grapes for Germany's white wines.

In the east, the butchers of Thuringia have perfected the art of sausage making—its fried sausages are sold around the country. Large poultry farms in Saxony rear geese for the traditional German Christmas dinner.

## The south

Hops are used to give beer its special flavor. People have been growing hops in Hallertau in Bavaria for more than a thousand years, and it is now the world's largest hop-growing area. Southern Germany also has orchards and vineyards. Apples are grown around Lindau, on the shores of Lake Constance.

The land of Baden-Württemberg is Germany's most southerly wine-growing area.

In mid-April, growers start to harvest the white asparagus. It thrives in the sandy soil of Baden-Württemberg. Asparagus is treated as a delicacy. During its short season, the restaurants all have special asparagus menus.

In the Saarland, in Germany's far west, plums are a specialty, particularly a variety called Zwetschgen or quetsches. They are made into large trays of juicy plum cake.

▽ *As soon as the snows melt*, temporary farmers take the cows up to the higher mountain pastures for the summer. The grass can recover in the valleys until the cows are taken back down in the fall.

In Franconia, the northern part of Bavaria, growers cultivate sweet cherries. Apples are made into juice and tasty apple strudel. People put cherries in a rich chocolate cake called Black Forest gateau. The West Allgäu in Bavaria is known for its cheeses.

## Fishing

Fishermen catch herrings, mackerel, cod, sardines, and shrimps in the North Sea, the Baltic, and the Atlantic. Fried fillets of plaice are a famous dish from Hamburg. Where rivers and lakes are less polluted, freshwater fish are increasing. Germans eat freshwater fish, such as trout, pike, carp, perch, and zander. Carp was once a favorite New Year's dish.

◁ **Cherry trees** are in full blossom in a wildflower meadow. Germany is one of the most important cherry producers. The fruits grow especially well in the west and south. Cherries are eaten as fruit and are used to make juices, cakes, and kirsch.

## COAST GUARDS

The North Sea dykes were built from clay and covered in grass hundreds of years ago. The coast guards keep "dyke sheep" to help maintain the dykes, which protect the land from high tides. The sheep trample down the soil without ripping up the grass and "mow" the grass by eating it.

## let's make...
# FRIED FLOUNDER

This dish comes from Finkenwerder, which is a part of the city of Hamburg in northern Germany. Fishing boats from here once went all over the North Sea and the Norwegian Sea.

### WHAT YOU NEED:

#### SERVES 4 PEOPLE:

4 flounders, gutted and ready
   to cook (each weighing
   about 12 ounces)
salt, white pepper
2–3 tablespoons plain flour
5 ounces bacon (optional)
⅓ cup butter
1 untreated organic lemon
fresh dill

### I CAN'T FIND ANY *flounder*

You can also make this dish with another flat fish, such as sole. Or use any other fish fillet.

### MY TIP

A tasty version of this recipe uses tiny North Sea shrimps. Fry these briefly with the bacon in butter. Then sprinkle them over the top of the flounder.

◁ This fish tastes great with almost any kind of potato dish. Try frying the potatoes with a few onion rings, or boil them in their skins, then peel them and add fresh parsley. Another great side dish is a cucumber salad.

**1** Thoroughly wash the flounder under cold water, then pat them dry with paper towels. Season them with salt and pepper, then dust each one thinly with flour on both sides.

**2** Use two wide skillets so you can cook all four fillets at the same time. Finely chop the bacon. Put half the bacon and half the butter into each skillet. Fry the bacon over medium heat until it is crispy.

**3** Put the flounder into the skillets side by side. Fry over medium heat for about 4 minutes, then turn over. Fry for 4 more minutes.

**4** With a fish slice carefully lift out the fillets so they don't fall apart. Put them on serving plates and decorate with lemon wedges and dill.

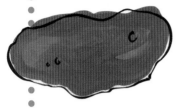

# let's make...
# POTATO PANCAKES

Potato pancakes are a specialty of the Rhineland, especially of Cologne. They are sold from stands at funfairs and festivals, and people eat them strolling along.

## WHAT YOU NEED:

### SERVES 4 PEOPLE:

2¼ lbs starchy potatoes
2 onions
just under ½ cup sour cream
4 eggs
about ¾ cup dried breadcrumbs
salt, black pepper
cooking oil for frying

◁ I love this pancake the traditional way, served with apple sauce. But my aunt prefers the savory version. She eats hers with smoked salmon.

### WHAT SORT OF _potatoes_?

Starchy potatoes work best for pancakes. Try Idaho, russet, or Yukon Gold potatoes.

### MY TIP

Try this pancake on a slice of pumpernickel, or black bread, with some golden syrup—this is the version loved in the hilly areas around Cologne.

**1** Wash and peel the potatoes, then grate them either finely or roughly—just as you prefer.

**2** Squeeze out the grated potatoes, either with your hands or in a clean kitchen cloth. Put the "dry" potato pulp into a bowl.

**3** Peel and finely grate the onions. Add them to the potatoes. Add the sour cream, eggs, breadcrumbs, some salt, and a little pepper. Stir or knead everything together.

**4** In a wide skillet, heat plenty of oil over medium heat. Use quite a bit of oil as the potatoes soak up a lot. **!**

**5** To make a pancake, put one heaped tablespoon of potato mix into the skillet. Pat it flat with the back of a large spoon. Fry the pancake for 3–4 minutes, then turn it over and fry for another 3–4 minutes, until both sides are crispy and golden brown. **!**

**6** Lift out finished pancakes and let them drain on paper towels while you cook the rest. Keep them warm in a low oven (200°F).

# let's make...
# DUMPLINGS AND MUSHROOMS

Dumplings can be made from bread, as in this recipe, or from potatoes. They are particularly popular in southern Germany, where people eat them with many sauce-based dishes.

▽ This Bavarian dish makes a great vegetarian meal, but it also tastes good with roast pork or goulash.

## WHAT YOU NEED:

### SERVES 4 PEOPLE:

5 stale bread rolls
salt
1 cup milk
½ bunch flat-leaved parsley

½ small onion
1 tablespoon butter
2 eggs

### FOR THE MUSHROOM SAUCE:

2 tablespoons dried
  mushrooms
4 onions
2 tablespoons butter
1 tablespoon plain flour
1 cup vegetable stock
½ cup light cream
2 teaspoons dried
  thyme
salt, black pepper

### SERVE WITH: mushroom sauce

Put the dried mushrooms in a small bowl, cover them with ½ cup warm water, and leave to soak. Drain and chop the mushrooms but keep the water. Peel and finely chop the onions. Heat the butter in a saucepan and fry the onions until golden. Add the mushrooms and fry for a few minutes. Dust with flour and fry for another minute, then pour in the stock. Add the soaking water and the cream. Season with thyme, salt, and pepper. Cook over gentle heat for 10 minutes.

**1** Cut the rolls into very thin slices and put them in a bowl. Sprinkle the slices with ¼ teaspoon salt. In a saucepan, bring the milk to a boil. Pour the milk over the rolls, cover with a clean cloth, and allow to soak for about 30 minutes.

**2** Meanwhile wash, pat dry, and finely chop the parsley. Peel and finely chop the onion *(see page 5)*. Melt the butter in a skillet and fry the onion until it is transparent (see-through). **!**

**3** Add the onions, parsley, and eggs to the soaked bread rolls. Knead everything with your hands until it is a smooth paste. With moist hands, shape the mixture into eight balls.

**4** In a large saucepan, bring plenty of water and 1 teaspoon salt to a boil. Reduce the heat and place the dumplings into the saucepan on a slotted spoon. Cook the dumplings over low heat for about 20 minutes. **!**

**5** Lift the dumplings out of the water with a slotted spoon and drain well. Serve with mushroom sauce.

# How we celebrate in
# GERMANY

People in Germany celebrate Christian holidays, the joys of summer, and the most important calendar dates.

*A*s in most western countries, Christian festivals, such as Easter and Christmas, are celebrated all over Germany. Many other religious Christian festivals are only celebrated in some federal areas. This depends on whether there are more Catholic or Protestant citizens in that area. New Year is celebrated everywhere.

## Rhine festivals

The summer festival known as "The Rhine in Flames" is a series of five huge firework displays on the Rhine River. They take place on different dates between May and September. The largest is celebrated in Koblenz on the second Saturday each August.

For each event, long convoys of seventy-five or more ships travel slowly up the Rhine, from Bingen to Bonn. Huge fireworks are set off from the ships. Bengal fires and laser light shows douse the towns and villages along its shore in colorful lights. Hundreds of thousands of people come to see the displays.

A similar event, known as "Cologne Lights," began in Cologne in 2001. Here the main two fireworks are set off from two large pontoon ships in the river. There are more fireworks on the shores. Music is played from huge speakers all along this stretch of the river. The fireworks explode in colors to match the rhythm of the music. When the convoy of ships arrives, people light 500,000 sparklers. The atmosphere is very festive.

## Silvester

Silvester is the name for New Year's Eve in Germany. At midnight, people set off even more fireworks, outside their homes in the street, outside bars, or in large open squares.

Donuts are a traditional food to eat on New Year's Eve. If people around Berlin make these themselves, they sometimes fill most with jam, but one with mustard. It is a challenge to see if everyone can eat their donut without letting on who had the mustard-filled bun!

For another custom, people melt a lump of lead over a candle. They throw the melted lead into a bowl of cold water. It sets firm in strange shapes, and everyone decides what these odd shapes look like. A little book tells people what this means for their future. If the shape looks like a lot of grass, for example, that means "lots of money."

◁ **Ships are lit** in festive colors as fireworks go off all around them on the Rhine River at Cologne—Cologne cathedral can be seen on the right. Live bands play on the shore, in time to the fireworks.

### BIG FESTIVAL

*The largest festival in the world is the Oktoberfest in Munich. It happens at the end of September. It is known as a beer festival, but there are many other events: festival parades, live brass bands, and fairground attractions.*

# Carnival

Carnival is the time before Lent, the time when Christians fast before Easter. It is celebrated all over Germany and known by many different names, including Karneval, Fastnacht, and Fasching.

The six days before Ash Wednesday is the time of the "street carnival." Everyone dresses in a funny costume, even the adults. There are parades with floats, marching bands, and dancers. People on the floats throw candies and bunches of flowers to the spectators.

The carnival clubs in each town elect their "rulers," often a prince and princess, for one season. There are many balls and so-called sessions, or shows. Comedians make speeches, and there are dance performances and many carnival songs for everyone to sing.

△ **The Prince** (with long pheasant feathers), the Peasant (with a fan of peacock feathers, and the Maid (not seen, a man in a woman's dress and with blond braids) "rule" in Cologne.

△ **May trees** decorate many houses on May 1. The tree is usually a birch, which has young leaves at this time of year. Ribbons are made from crepe paper or silk. They are in many colors that once had special meanings.

## May Day

May 1 is Labor Day in Germany and a national holiday. Labor unions organize processions and speeches on that day. But there are many other traditions connected with that day.

The night before, April 30, is Walpurgisnacht, the night of the witches. Traditionally, people had bonfires to burn the "bad spirits." Today, people sing and dance together through the night, the so-called "dance into May."

In southern Germany, people parade with a brass band to the village square. There they put up a *Maibaum*, or May tree. This is a tall pole or fir tree from which colorful ribbons hang. People hold the other end of the ribbons and sing and dance around the May pole.

In other areas, people hang a May tree outside their homes. This is a tree or branch, often a birch, that is beautifully decorated with colorful ribbons. In the past, young men put a May tree outside the window of their beloved. It was left their for a month. Then the young woman let her admirer know if she liked him too. Today, people hang up these colorful trees as joyful decorations for their houses and to welcome the spring.

# let's make...
# CHRISTMAS STOLLEN

There are many recipes for Stollen. Some have a marzipan filling, some are made with poppy seeds. The famous Dresden stollen is made with quark, a German soft cheese.

## WHAT YOU NEED:

### MAKES 1 STOLLEN:

2 cups ricotta cheese
(or 1 lb fresh cream
cheese plus 3 tablespoons
buttermilk)
½ cup softened butter
1 pinch salt
¾ cup white sugar
1 teaspoon vanilla extract
2 eggs

1 teaspoon grated zest
from an untreated
lemon
½ cup soft dried apricots
½ cup raisins
⅓ cup shelled pistachios
½ cup chopped almonds
4 cups all-purpose plain flour
4 teaspoons baking powder

### PLUS:

flour for the work surface
⅛ cup butter for brushing
⅔ cup confectioners'

sugar for sprinkling

◁ One slice of this
cake is never
enough for me!

### WHY DOES THIS CAKE HAVE A _dent?_

Traditionally, this Christmas cake is made by folding the dough over and over. This is why it has a dent. The folding symbolizes the swaddling clothes of the baby Jesus.

**1** Put the ricotta cheese into a fine sieve and drain for about 20 minutes. Heat the oven to 350°F. Line a baking tray with baking paper.

**2** Put the butter, salt, sugar, vanilla extract, and eggs into a bowl and beat with a handheld mixer until foamy. Knead in the ricotta cheese. Finely chop and add the apricots, raisins, pistachios, almonds, and lemon zest.

**3** In a separate bowl, mix the baking powder into the flour. Beat this mixture into the cheese mixture, a bit at a time. Knead until you have a smooth dough. Add a little more flour if necessary—the dough should be smooth, soft, and elastic, not sticky.

**4** On a floured surface, shape the dough into a loaf with a lengthways dent running down the center. Place the loaf on a baking tray. Bake in the center of the oven for about 1 hour.

**5** Melt the butter. Take the stollen out of the oven and brush with the butter. Thickly sprinkle the cake with confectioners' sugar and allow to cool on a rack.

# let's make...
# MUTZENMANDELN

Mutzenmandeln are a favorite carnival pastry. Like pancakes on Shrove Tuesday or Mardi Gras, people make these little cookies to use up eggs and fat before the start of Lent.

▽ At my last carnival party, Dad dressed up as a clown and brought freshly baked Mutzenmandeln for us all.

## WHAT YOU NEED:

### MAKES ABOUT 50 MUTZENMANDELN:

2 cups plain flour
½ cup shelled and ground almonds
1 teaspoon baking powder
3 eggs
1 stick cold butter

1 pinch salt
a pinch each of ground cinnamon, ground cardamom, and grated lemon zest

### PLUS:

oil for deep-frying
confectioners' sugar for dusting

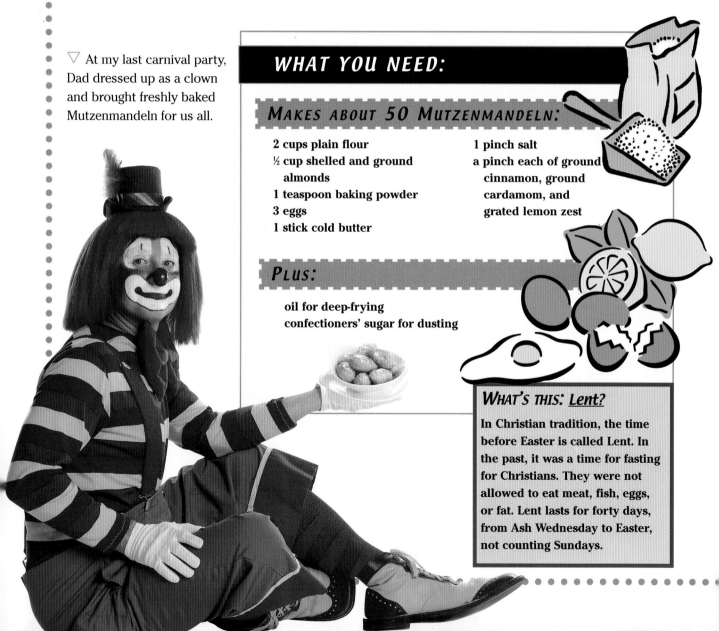

### WHAT'S THIS: Lent?

In Christian tradition, the time before Easter is called Lent. In the past, it was a time for fasting for Christians. They were not allowed to eat meat, fish, eggs, or fat. Lent lasts for forty days, from Ash Wednesday to Easter, not counting Sundays.

**1** In a bowl, stir together the flour, almonds, and baking powder. Add the eggs, butter, and the spices and knead to a smooth dough.

**2** Shape the dough into a ball. Wrap it in plastic wrap and chill for at least 1 hour in the fridge.

**3** Heat the oil for deep-frying. Hold a wooden spoon into the fat. If the bubbles rise on the stem immediately, the fat is hot enough.

**4** Using two teaspoons, take a small portion of dough from the ball and form it into an almond shape. Deep-fry a few at a time in the hot fat for about 1–2 minutes, until they are a golden brown color. Lift the Mutzenmandeln out with a slotted spoon and drain them on paper towels. Sprinkle them with confectioners' sugar and allow to cool.

# How we celebrate at home in
# GERMANY

**F**amily celebrations are very important in Germany. Families are often small, with only one or two children. So people like to celebrate with all their relatives if they can—aunts, uncles, cousins, and grandparents.

## Christmas

Germany is world-famous for its Christmas celebrations. Many customs that are now common in other countries came originally from Germany.

The four weeks before Christmas are called *Advent*. Children have calendars with a countdown to Christmas. Each day until December 24 they open one door, and often there are chocolates inside. The family has an advent wreath of pine twigs and cones with four candles. Four Sundays before Christmas they light one candle, three Sundays before they light two, until all are lit the last Sunday before Christmas Day. When the candles are lit, the family sit together and eat their *stollen*, a Christmas cake.

◁ **Santa Claus** comes on Christmas Eve. He knocks on the door as most German houses do not have a chimney for him to slide down. Often he reads from a golden book that tells him whether a child has been good or not.

Most towns have a Christmas market, and large towns even have several markets. There people can buy gifts, decorations for their Christmas trees, candles, handmade toys, candies, and cakes.

Christmas trees in Germany are usually real pine trees. In the past, people stuck real candles to the branches on special candlesticks. Today fewer people do this because of the fire risks. Festive lights adorn the stores, but normally not people's homes and front yards.

## Children's days

German families celebrate Christian events in a child's life. Most children are baptized, often very soon after birth. Between the ages of six and twelve, Catholic children receive their first communion. Protestant children are confirmed after two years of afternoon classes at church when they are fourteen.

An important day in every child's life is the first day at school. The parents and other relatives accompany the child to school. After the first lessons, the child is given a *Schultüte* (say "shool-toote"). This is a large cardboard cone filled with candies and toys.

▽ *The first day at school* is an important day in a child's life. To "sweeten" this start of a life of learning, children are given a cone filled with candies and other gifts by their parents or grandparents.

## ST. MARTIN

St. Martin was a Roman soldier and later the bishop of Tours. He was a kind man—legend tells us that he cut his coat in half to share it with a beggar in a snow storm. Today, the saint is remembered on the evening of November 11. German children carry paper lanterns with lit candles in a procession. They knock on people's doors and sing special St. Martin's songs. As a reward they are given candies.

## Easter

Many Easter traditions come from Germany originally. People celebrate with painted Easter eggs and chocolate bunnies. Children help paint the eggs. Branches of trees with spring leaves are hung with decorated eggs. Often the parents hide little nests with candies in the garden or home. The children get up early on Sunday morning to try and find them.

Some traditional foods are eaten for Easter. Maundy Thursday is known as *Gründonnerstag* or green Thursday, and so people eat green foods, such as Savoy cabbage. The main Good Friday meal is fish, and on Easter Sunday people often eat lamb.

△ **For their birthdays**, people often invite family and friends around in the afternoon. They have coffee or hot chocolate and a big creamy birthday cake.

## Kaffee und Kuchen

When people in Germany get together, they invite each other for *Kaffee und Kuchen*, or coffee and cake. The cake may be bought at a patisserie. But many people bake their own cakes, fruit tarts, and cookies. For family birthdays, especially, a birthday cake is baked and presented to the person whose birthday it is. Coffee and cake are taken in the afternoon. Often people use their best china.

# Weddings

German couples do not traditionally have a bachelor or a bachelorette party. Instead, they spend the evening before the wedding at the bride's home. Friends and neighbors come and smash their old china on the stairs. The couple has to sweep up the shards. The noise is meant to chase away bad spirits, and tidying up together prepares the couple for a lifetime of working together when they are married.

At the wedding party, relatives may kidnap the bride and take her to a nearby bar. Once the bridegroom has noticed that his new wife is missing, he goes to find her. As a "ransom" he pays for everything the bride and her abductors have eaten or drunk in the meantime.

## TURKISH SANTA

*Many Turkish families in Germany also celebrate Christmas. They buy a Christmas tree and gifts for each other even though Christmas is not a Muslim festival. But it is not Santa Claus who brings the gifts. Instead it is Noel Baba, and he comes on New Year's Eve.*

▽ **Polterabend**, or "noisy evening," is the evening before a wedding. Friends come and smash their old china. The couple sweep it up together, but a mischievous friend may empty the trash can again and again!

# let's make...
# SAUERBRATEN

This marinated pot roast is our family's favorite Sunday meal. It takes a few days to make so we don't eat it every day. We often eat it with potato dumplings and red cabbage.

## WHAT YOU NEED:

### SERVES 4-6 PEOPLE:

1 onion
1 carrot
1 stick celery
1 cup wine vinegar
5 cloves
½ teaspoon allspice berries
1 teaspoon juniper berries
2½ lbs pot roast of beef
2 tablespoons lard or oil
3 ounces gingerbread pieces
1–2 handfuls raisins
1–3 tablespoons golden syrup
½ carton crème fraîche
salt, black pepper

◁ On Sundays, we all sit together and enjoy this dish. My parents thought it was great when I made sauerbraten all by myself.

### WHAT'S THIS: sauerbraten?

Literally, this means "sour roast," because the meat is marinated in a sour liquid, with lots of vinegar. In the past, when people had no fridges, that was a way of preserving meat. It also makes tough cuts of meat very tender.

**1** Peel the onion and carrot. Trim the celery. Roughly chop all three and put them in a saucepan. Add the vinegar, 2½ cups water, the cloves, and the allspice and juniper berries. Bring to a boil. Turn off the heat and allow to cool.

**!**

**2** Wash the meat under cold water and place it in a narrow, high bowl. Pour over the vinegar mixture. Make sure the meat is completely covered with the liquid. Cover the bowl with a clean cloth and place it in the fridge for 3–4 days to marinate. Turn the meat over several times during this period.

**3** On the day you want to eat the beef, heat the oil in a large Dutch oven. Lift the meat out of the liquid and pat it dry with paper towels. Place it in the oil and fry all around on a high heat to seal. Add half a glass of water to the saucepan. In a sieve, filter about 1 cup vinegar marinade and add. Cover and cook over low heat for 1½ hours.

**!**

**!**

**4** Lift out the meat, cover, and keep warm. Finely crumble the gingerbread or pumpernickel into the sauce and stir. Stir in the raisins, syrup, and crème fraîche. Season with pepper and salt. Serve the meat with the sauce.

# let's make...
# PLUM CAKE

In summer, when lots of fruits ripen, this is one of the nicest ways of using them up. Mom makes plum cake for all summer birthdays—it's large enough for any number of candles!

▽ My grandparents, aunt, and uncle are coming over this afternoon for cake and coffee, to celebrate Dad's birthday. I can't wait!

## WHAT YOU NEED:

### MAKES 20 SLICES:

2 cups all-purpose flour
1 teaspoon powdered
   easy-blend yeast
½ cup lukewarm milk
1 tablespoon sugar
1 pinch salt
1 egg yolk
1½ tablespoons soft butter
4 lbs firm plums

### PLUS:

flour for the work surface
butter for the baking tray
1 cup almond slices

### WHAT SORT OF _plums?_

The original recipe uses quetsches, a kind of damson plum. But there are many other types of plums to choose from. They range in size from cherry to apple, and in color from yellow, green, and red to purple. Choose firm plums that have a juicy flavor and do not contain too much water.

**1** Put the flour in a bowl and stir in the yeast and pour over the milk. Sprinkle over a little sugar and flour. Cover with a clean cloth and stand in a warm place for 15 minutes, until the flour has cracks on the surface.

**2** Add the salt, egg yolk, and soft butter. Using the kneading hooks of a handheld blender, work it all into a smooth dough. It should easily come away from the bowl and not be sticky.

**3** Quickly knead the dough with your hands on a floured surface. Shape it into a ball, dust with flour, cover, and allow to rise again in a warm place, until it has become almost twice as big.

**5** Knead the dough again, then roll it out on a floured surface. Grease the baking tray with a little butter. Lift the dough onto the tray and press and push it out to the edges.

**4** Wash the plums and halve them or fold them open. Cut out the pits. Heat the oven to 400°F.

**6** Place the plums closely together on the dough. Sprinkle over the almonds. Bake in the center of the oven for about 30 minutes.

# How we live in
# GERMANY

**G**ermany is a diverse country, and the people who live there follow many different lifestyles. One thing most people have in common is a love of the outdoors, sports, and vacations.

## Parks and gardens

In most German towns there are lovely parks, and people love going for a walk in the park. Turkish families in Germany often get together in the park in large groups to have a picnic and barbecue. The parks also attract joggers, dog walkers, and children who play in the playgrounds. Many Germans have a yard behind their house or they rent a piece of land elsewhere. They grow beautiful flowers and many gardens have a fish pond. In summer, people invite friends for a barbecue. Gardening is a popular hobby, especially for older people.

▽ **Boat excursions** are a favorite entertainment. Cruise ships go up and down Germany's many rivers, such as the Rhine, Danube, or Moselle. Evening tours often include music and shows.

△ **Snow falls** in many parts of Germany in winter so everyone can enjoy themselves with snowball fights, making snowmen, tobogganing, ice skating, ice hockey, skiing, and snowboarding.

## Sports

Germans are sports mad. One in every three Germans belongs to a sports club. Their greatest passion is soccer; Germany won the World Cup in 1954, 1974, and 1990. It hosted the games in 2006. Every village has its club, and people are fiercely loyal to their local club. Another very popular sport is tennis.

There are also swimming pools, both indoor and open-air, in almost every village. People cycle and hike, and inline skating is popular. All kinds of winter sports, including ski jumping, also have many fans. Millions tune in to sports events on TV, from soccer matches to motor racing and boxing.

## Family life

In large cities, Germans live in apartments in rows of houses. In villages, they may live in a bungalow or a two-family house. Often people rent and do not own their homes.

For breakfast, German families often have a great spread of different foods, especially on Sundays, when no one has to rush off to work or school. There are bowls of cereals and different kinds of bread, including rolls, country breads, and sweet loaves. There are different cold meats, hams, and cheeses, all sorts of jams, and boiled eggs.

△ **Hiking trails** make it possible to walk long or short distances anywhere in Germany. People enjoy walking in the hilly mountain regions, climbing the higher peaks, or paddling in the mudflats of the North Sea.

People used to have their main meal at lunchtime. In some families this still happens, because children get home from school at this time. But in many families today both parents work, so the main meal is eaten in the evening. The meal can be a pot roast of meat, for example a "false hare." Other favorites are sausages or meat rissoles—burgers without buns.

The many ethnic groups in Germany have introduced their own dishes, and German children enjoy Italian pasta dishes and pizzas as well as Turkish doner kabobs or gyros. *Fritten*, or fries, are everyone's favorite.

For dessert people have a blancmange, ice cream, or a red dessert called *grütze*. Many Germans today eat fast foods, such as burgers, just like in other Western countries.

# School and vacation

Children in Germany start school at the age of six. They attend elementary school for four years. After that, they visit one of three types of schools. *Hauptschule* (grades 5–9) generally leads to a vocational (or skill-based) school and an apprenticeship. *Realschule* (grades 5–10) is a higher vocational school. *Gymnasium* (grades 5–13) ends with the *Abitur*. This is the certificate students need to enter college.

The school day starts at 8 A.M. and finishes at 1 or 2 P.M. Children do not eat at school. They have lots of homework to complete at home and very few after-school activities. All children learn English.

▽ **Zoo animals** are important personalities in Germany. Baby animals, like Marlar, the smallest of the elephants below, may even become celebrities. A visit to the zoo is a big draw.

## SAVING THE ENVIRONMENT

Germans recycle much of their trash. They pay a deposit and return bottles and cans, and they collect paper, plastic, and metal in recycling trash cans.

Kitchen and garden waste is composted in the yard. Instead of using plastic carrier bags, people bring their own, made from cotton.

## let's make...
# FALSE HARE

This is an old-fashioned children's favorite, and it is not really a hare, but a meatloaf with a hidden surprise! Every region in Germany has its own version, some include sausages too.

## WHAT YOU NEED:

### SERVES 4 PEOPLE:

3 eggs
2 slices toast
1½ lbs mixed ground meat
  (half beef, half pork)
salt, black pepper
2 teaspoons dried oregano
3 tablespoons oil
½ cup broth

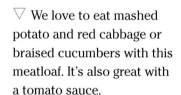 ▽ We love to eat mashed potato and red cabbage or braised cucumbers with this meatloaf. It's also great with a tomato sauce.

### WHY IS IT CALLED _false hare?_

Perhaps it was because people pretended that they had a real hare for Sunday lunch. Many German recipes have names that promise something they do not keep—Heaven and Earth, for example is a potato mash with fried liver and apple stew; and _halver hahn_, half a chicken, is in fact just a cheese sandwich!

**1** Prick two of the eggs on both ends with a needle. Then place them carefully (with a spoon) into a saucepan of boiling water. Cover and boil for 10 minutes until they are hard. Rinse under cold water and shell.

**2** Place the toast in a bowl. Pour over some warm water and allow to swell. Squeeze out the bread and put it in a bowl. Add the ground meat and crack in the third egg. Season with salt, pepper, and oregano. Knead the mixture thoroughly with your hands.

**3** Rinse your hands under cold water, then shape the meat mixture into an oval loaf shape. Flatten the loaf and set the shelled eggs on top. Fold the meat around the eggs so they are completely enclosed.

**4** Heat the oil in a Dutch oven. Add the meatloaf. Fry and turn it for 5 minutes to brown it all over. Turn it carefully, with two spoons, so it won't fall apart. Pour in about ½ cup broth. Cover with a lid, reduce the heat, and cook over low heat for 40 minutes. Turn the loaf a couple of times.

# let's make...
# SAUSAGES &
# SAUERKRAUT

Sausages are a typical midweek supper dish, but they are also everyone's favorite at a Sunday barbecue. You can find them on stands at Christmas markets or at funfairs too.

## WHAT YOU NEED:

### SERVES 4-6 PEOPLE:

1 onion
1 tablespoon lard or cooking oil (plus more oil for frying)
1½ lbs sauerkraut
1 cup apple juice
3 juniper berries
salt, black pepper
24 Nuremberg roasting sausages (approx 1 ounce each; or 4–6 large sausages)

◁ There are about 1,500 different types of sausages in Germany! I love the ones from Nuremberg best.

### WHAT'S THIS: sauerkraut?

This is a sliced and fermented (soured) cabbage. It is popular in Germany and Poland.

### MY TIP

Sausages are great with tomato ketchup or mustard. In Berlin, people eat them with a curry sauce—that's ketchup with curry powder stirred in. Delicious!

**1** Peel and chop the onion *(see page 5)*. In a saucepan heat the lard or oil. Add the onion and fry for 5 minutes over medium heat, until the onion is transparent (see-through).

**2** Add the sauerkraut and fork through with two forks to loosen it. Then pour in the apple juice and stir in the juniper berries. Season with salt and pepper, and cook uncovered over low heat for about 30 minutes.

**3** While the sauerkraut is cooking, heat a little oil in a skillet (or light a barbecue). Add the sausages and cook over medium heat for about 10 minutes. Turn them a few times to ensure they are browned evenly all over.

**4** Serve the sauerkraut with the sausages and some mashed potatoes or potato salad.

# let's make...
# RED GROATS

Everyone just loves this fruit dessert. You can find it in the simplest homes and in the most expensive restaurants. Originally, it comes from northern Germany.

## WHAT YOU NEED:

### MAKES 8 PORTIONS:

1 lb 2 ounces redcurrants
4 ounces sour cherries
4 ounces raspberries
½ lb strawberries
2–4 tablespoons sugar

1½ cups redcurrant
  or cherry nectar
1 cinnamon stick
2 tablespoons cornstarch

### FOR THE SAUCE:

2 vanilla pods
3½ cups milk
2 tablespoons sugar
1½ tablespoons
  cornstarch
2 egg yolks
½ cup whipping
  or heavy cream

◁ Originally, this recipe was always made using only red fruits, but I've made a green version with gooseberries and kiwis, and my brother made a yellow one with peaches and pineapple.

## WHAT'S THIS: groats?

*Rote grütze*, or red groats, was originally made with crushed grains called groats and fruit juice. This version is still cooked in eastern Europe. But today a much lighter version is made with cornstarch and fresh fruit, and this is popular everywhere.

**1** Wash the redcurrants and pull them off their stalks with a fork. Wash the cherries; remove the stalks and pits. Don't wash the raspberries but pick over and throw away any that are moldy. Wash the strawberries, pull off the green stems, and cut the fruits in halves or fourths, if they are large.

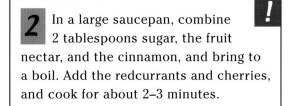

**2** In a large saucepan, combine 2 tablespoons sugar, the fruit nectar, and the cinnamon, and bring to a boil. Add the redcurrants and cherries, and cook for about 2–3 minutes. !

**3** In a bowl, stir the cornstarch into a little cold water. Stir this into the saucepan. Cook and stir until the mixture begins to thicken. !

**4** Now add in the raspberries and strawberries. Add sugar to taste, stir, then let the mixture cool. !

**6** Take the saucepan off the heat. In a bowl, whisk together the egg yolks and the cream. Pour this mixture into the vanilla milk. Don't boil it again. Allow to cool. !

**5** Meanwhile slit open the vanilla pods and scrape out the seeds. In a saucepan, bring the seeds, pods, milk, and sugar to a boil. In a bowl, stir the cornstarch into a little water until smooth. Add this to the milk and cook briefly until it thickens.

# Look it up
# GERMANY

**advent** the four weeks before Christmas; German children have countdown advent calendars and families lights candles on their advent wreaths

**carnival** the time before Lent; marked by wearing costumes and masks, joining processions, and many celebrations

**dirndl** traditional folk clothes of a woman in Bavaria; a dress, blouse, and apron

**groats** a hulled and crushed cereal

**kaffee und kuchen** coffee and cake; a favorite German afternoon meal

**lederhosen** traditional folk clothes for a man in Bavaria; shorts or three-quarter-length trousers made from leather

**Lent** the period of fasting before Easter for devout Christians

**mutzenmandeln** a favorite cookie baked and eaten during carnival

**Oktoberfest** a beer festival in Munich; the largest festival in the world

**polterabend** the eve of a wedding in Germany; friends smash their old china on the couple's doorstep, and the couple has to sweep up the shards

**sauerbraten** a pickled pot roast of beef; the meat is marinated in a vinegar sauce for several days; originally sauerbraten was made with horse meat

**sauerkraut** a pickled cabbage; can be eaten hot or cold

**St. Martin** (316–397 CE) a Roman soldier and later the Bishop of Tours in France; known as the patron saint of France; his acts of kindness are celebrated by lantern processions on November 11 in Germany

**stollen** a German Christmas cake; it is shaped with a dent down its length, to resemble the swaddling clothes of the baby Jesus

# Find out more
# GERMANY

## Books to read

Amos, Janine.
**Getting to Know Germany and German.**
Barron's Educational Series: 1993.

Lord, Richard, and McKay, Susan.
**Germany (Festivals of the World).**
Gareth Stevens Publishing: 1997.

Sheen, Barbara.
**Foods of Germany.**
KidHaven Press: 2006.

Heinrichs Gray, Susan. **Germany
(True Books).** Children's Press, CT: 2003.

Lane, Kathryn. **Germany – the Land,
the People, the Culture.**
Crabtree Publishing Company: 2001.

## Web sites to check out

**www.germany.info/relaunch/culture/life/
G_Kids/index.htm**
The kids' pages of the Web site of the
German Embassy in Washington, D.C.

**www.cia.gov/library/publications/the-
world-factbook/geos/gm.html**
The CIA's site with information, facts, and
figures about Germany

**www.germanculture.com.ua**
A site all about German culture, history,
sports, and daily life, with lots of
information on food and festivals

**www.globalgourmet.com/destinations/
germany**
All about food in northern, central, and
southern Germany, festivals and feasts

**www.travelsthroughgermany.com/
website2/germanfood.htm**
Recipes and feature articles on German
food and culture

# Index

# GERMANY